CAPE POETRY PAPERBACKS

DEREK WALCOTT
THE CASTAWAY
AND OTHER POEMS

Dear Zee-Bee,
        Lovely poetry for a
lovely girl.
        Happy birthday and many
more.

        Lotsa Love,
        Greg.

Derek Walcott

THE CASTAWAY
AND OTHER POEMS

JONATHAN CAPE
THIRTY BEDFORD SQUARE LONDON

FIRST PUBLISHED 1965
REISSUED IN THIS FORMAT 1969
REPRINTED 1972
© 1963, 1964, 1965 BY DEREK WALCOTT

JONATHAN CAPE LTD
30 BEDFORD SQUARE, LONDON WCI

ISBN 0 224 61772 9

Condition of Sale

This book is sold subject to the condition that it
shall not, by way of trade or otherwise, be lent,
re-sold, hired out, or otherwise circulated without the publisher's prior consent, in any form of
binding or cover other than that in which it
is published and without a similar condition
including this condition being imposed on the
subsequent purchaser.

Printed in Great Britain by
Fletcher & Son Ltd, Norwich
and bound by
Richard Clay (The Chaucer Press) Ltd, Bungay, Suffolk

Contents

Acknowledgments

Some of these poems have appeared in the *London Magazine*, *Spectator*, *Encounter*, the *Beloit Poetry Journal*, the *Review of English Literature* and the *Borestone Mountain Poetry Awards*, *1963*.

for John Hearne

The Castaway

The starved eye devours the seascape for the morsel
Of a sail.

The horizon threads it infinitely.

Action breeds frenzy. I lie,
Sailing the ribbed shadow of a palm,
Afraid lest my own footprints multiply.

Blowing sand, thin as smoke,
Bored, shifts its dunes.
The surf tires of its castles like a child.

The salt green vine with yellow trumpet-flower,
A net, inches across nothing.
Nothing: the rage with which the sandfly's head is filled.

Pleasures of an old man:
Morning: contemplative evacuation, considering
The dried leaf, nature's plan.

In the sun, the dog's faeces
Crusts, whitens like coral.
We end in earth, from earth began.
In our own entrails, genesis.

If I listen I can hear the polyp build,
The silence thwanged by two waves of the sea.
Cracking a sea-louse, I make thunder split.

Godlike, annihilating godhead, art
And self, I abandon
Dead metaphors: the almond's leaf-like heart,

The ripe brain rotting like a yellow nut
Hatching
Its babel of sea-lice, sandfly and maggot,

That green wine bottle's gospel choked with sand,
Labelled, a wrecked ship,
Clenched seawood nailed and white as a man's hand.

The Swamp

Gnawing the highway's edges, its black mouth
Hums quietly: 'Home, come home ...'

Behind its viscous breath the very word 'growth'
Grows fungi, rot;
White mottling its root.

More dreaded
Than canebrake, quarry, or sun-shocked gully-bed
Its horrors held Hemingway's hero rooted
To sure, clear shallows.

It begins nothing. Limbo of cracker convicts, Negroes.
Its black mood
Each sunset takes a smear of your life's blood.

Fearful, original sinuosities! Each mangrove sapling
Serpentlike, its roots obscene
As a six-fingered hand,

Conceals within its clutch the mossbacked toad,
Toadstools, the potent ginger-lily,
Petals of blood,

The speckled vulva of the tiger-orchid;
Outlandish phalloi
Haunting the travellers of its one road.

Deep, deeper than sleep
Like death,
Too rich in its decrescence, too close of breath,

In the fast-filling night, note
How the last bird drinks darkness with its throat,
How the wild saplings slip

Backward to darkness, go black
With widening amnesia, take the edge
Of nothing to them slowly, merge

Limb, tongue and sinew into a knot
Like chaos, like the road
Ahead.

Dogstar

The dogstar's rabid. Our street
burns its spilt garbage. Spent with heat
I brood on three good friends
dead in one year,
one summer's shock,
here where summer never ends.
I shall meet them there, I shall meet them there!

Beyond the window where I work
a neighbour's child
doubled in glass
seems to be walking among cloud,
below her feet
the flames of grass
are fuelled by their burning blood.
The dog, the dog will have its meat!

Sweat-drenched, muttering aloud,
I see a childhood uncle, mad, now dead,
sweating to whittle a cane stalk, a bead
jewels his forehead like the toad.
I cannot put day's burning smell aside
like a new book I am too tired to read.

Shovelled in like sticks to feed earth's raging oven,
consumed like heretics in this poem's pride,
these clouds, their white smoke, make and unmake heaven.

The Flock

The grip of winter tightening, its thinned
volleys of blue-wing teal and mallard fly
from the longbows of reeds bent by the wind,
arrows of yearning for our different sky.
A season's revolution hones their sense,
whose target is our tropic light, while I
awoke this sunrise to a violence
of images migrating from the mind.
Skeletal forest, a sepulchral knight
riding in silence at a black tarn's edge
hooves cannonading snow
in the white funeral of the year,
antlike across the forehead of an alp
in iron contradiction crouched
against those gusts that urge the mallards south.
Vizor'd with blind defiance of his quest,
its yearly divination of the spring.
I travel through such silence, making dark
symbols with this pen's print across snow,
measuring winter's augury by words
settling the branched mind like migrating birds,
and never question when they come or go.

The style, tension of motion and the dark,
inflexible direction of the world
as it revolves upon its centuries
with change of language, climate, customs, light,
with our own prepossession day by day

year after year with images of flight,
survive our condemnation and the sun's
exultant larks.
    The dark, impartial Arctic
whose glaciers encased the mastodon,
froze giant minds in marble attitudes
revolves with tireless, determined grace
upon an iron axle, though the seals
howl with inhuman cries across its ice
and pages of torn birds are blown across
whitening tundras like engulfing snow.

Till its annihilation may the mind
reflect his fixity through winter, tropic,
until that equinox when the clear eye
clouds, like a mirror, without contradiction,
greet the black wings that cross it as a blessing
like the high, whirring flock that flew across
the cold sky of this page when I began
this journey by the wintry flare of dawn,
flying by instinct to their secret places
both for their need and for my sense of season.

A Village Life

(for John Robertson)

I

Through the wide, grey loft window,
I watched that winter morning, my first snow
crusting the sill, puzzle the black,
nuzzling tom. Behind my back
a rime of crud glazed my cracked coffee-cup,
a snowfall of torn poems piling up
heaped by a rhyming spade.
Starved, on the prowl,
I was a frightened cat in that grey city.
I floated, a cat's shadow, through the black wool
sweaters, leotards and parkas of the fire-haired,
snow-shouldered Greenwich Village mädchen,
homesick, my desire
crawled across snow
like smoke, for its lost fire.

All that winter I haunted
your house on Hudson Street, a tiring friend,
demanding to be taken in, drunk, and fed.
I thought winter would never end.

I cannot imagine you dead.

But that stare, frozen,
a frosted pane in sunlight,
gives nothing back by letting nothing in,
your kindness or my pity.

No self-reflection lies
within those silent, ice-blue irises,
whose image is some snow-locked mountain lake
in numb Montana.

And since that winter I have learnt to gaze
on life indifferently as through a pane of glass.

II

Your image rattled on the subway glass
is my own death-mask in an overcoat;
under New York, the subterranean freight
of human souls, locked in an iron cell,
station to station cowed with swaying calm,
thunders to its end, each in its private hell,
each plumped, prime bulk still swinging by its arm
upon a hook. You're two years dead. And yet
I watch that silence spreading through our souls:
that horn-rimmed midget who consoles
his own deformity with Sartre on Genet.
Terror still eats the nerves, the Word
is gibberish, the plot Absurd.
The turnstile slots, like addicts, still consume
obols and aspirin, Charon in his grilled cell
grows vague about our crime, our destination.
Not all are silent, or endure
the enormity of silence; at one station,
somewhere off 33rd and Lexington,
a fur-wrapped matron screamed above the roar
of rattling iron. Nobody took her on,
We looked away. Such scenes
rattle our trust in nerves tuned like machines.
All drives as you remember it, the pace
of walking, running the rat race,
locked in a system, ridden by its rail,
within a life where no one dares to fail.
I watch your smile breaking across my skull,
the hollows of your face below my face

sliding across it like a pane of glass.
Nothing endures. Even in his cities
man's life is grass.
Times Square. We sigh and let off steam,
who should screech with the braking wheels, scream
like our subway-Cassandra, heaven-sent
to howl for Troy, emerge
blind from the blast of daylight, whirled
apart like papers from a vent.

III

Going away, through Queen's we pass
a cemetery of miniature skyscrapers. The verge
blazes its rust, its taxi-yellow leaves. It's fall.
I stare through glass,
my own reflection there, at
empty avenues, lawns, spires, quiet
stones, where the curb's rim
wheels westward, westward, where thy bones ...

Montana, Minnesota, your real
America, lost in tall grass, serene idyll.

A Tropical Bestiary

IBIS
Flare of the ibis, rare vermilion,
A hieroglyphic of beak-headed Egypt
That haunts, they claim, the green swamp-traveller
Who catches it to watch its plumage fade,
Loses its colours in captivity,
Blanches into a pinkish, stilted heron
Among the garrulous fishwife gulls, bitterns and spoonbills
And ashen herons of the heronry.
She never pines, complains at being kept,
Yet, imperceptibly, fades from her fire,
Pointing no moral but the fact
Of flesh that has lost pleasure in the act,
Of domesticity, drained of desire.

OCTOPUS
Post coitum, omne animal ... from love
The eight limbs loosen, like tentacles in water,
Like the slow tendrils of
The octopus.
          Fathoms down
They drift, numbed by the shock
Of an electric charge, drown
Vague as lidless fishes, separate
Like the anemone from rock
The sleek eel from its sea-cleft, drawn
By the darkening talons of the tide.
Pulse of the sea in the locked, heaving side.

LIZARD

Fear:
    the heraldic lizard, magnified,
Devouring its midge.
        Last night I plucked
'as a brand from the burning', a murderous, pincered beetle
Floundering in urine like a shipwreck shallop
Rudderless, its legs frantic as oars.
Did I, by this act, set things right side up?
It was not death I dreaded but the fight
With nothing. The aged, flailing their claws
On flowery coverlets, may dread such salvation,
The impotence of rescue or compassion.
Rightening a beetle damns creation.
It may have felt more terror on its back
When my delivering fingers, huge as hell,
Shadowed the stiffening victim with their jaws
Than the brown lizard, Galapagos-large,
Waggling its horny tail at morning's morsel
Held for the midge.
        Mercy has strange laws.
Withdraw and leave the scheme of things in charge.

MAN O' WAR BIRD

The idling pivot of the frigate bird
Sways the world's scales, tilts cobalt sea and sky,
Rightens, by its round eye, my drift
Through heaven when I shift
My study of the sun.
        The easy wings
Depend upon the stress I give such things
As my importance to its piercing height, the peace
Of its slow, ravening circuit of a speck
Upon a beach prey to its beak
Like any predatory tern it seizes.
In that blue wildfire somewhere is an Eye
That weighs this world exactly as it pleases.

SEA CRAB

The sea crab's cunning, halting, awkward grace
is the syntactical envy of my hand;
obliquity burrowing to surface
from hot, plain sand.
Those who require vision, complexity,
tire of its distressing
limits: sea, sand, scorching sky.
Cling to this ground, though constellations race,
the horizon burn, the wave coil, hissing,
salt sting the eye.

THE WHALE, HIS BULWARK

To praise the blue whale's crystal jet,
To write, 'O fountain!' honouring a spout
Provokes this curse:
         'The high are humbled yet'
From those who humble Godhead, beasthood, verse.

Once, the Lord raised this bulwark to our eyes,
Once, in our seas, whales threshed,
The harpooner was common. Once, I heard
Of a baleine beached up the Grenadines, fleshed
By derisive, antlike villagers: a prize
Reduced from majesty to pygmy-size.
Salt-crusted, mythological,
And dead.

The boy who told me couldn't believe his eyes,
And I believed him. When I was small
God and a foundered whale were possible.
Whales are rarer, God as invisible.
Yet, through His gift, I praise the unfathomable,
Though the boy may be dead, the praise unfashionable,
The tale apocryphal.

TARPON

At Cedros, thudding the dead sand
in spasms, the tarpon
gaped with a gold eye, drowned
thickly, thrashing with brute pain
this sea I breathe.
Stilled, its bulk,
screwed to the eye's lens, slowly
sought design. It dried like silk,
leisurely, altered to lead.
The belly, leprous, silver, bulged
like a cold chancre for the blade.
Suddenly it shuddered in immense
doubt, but the old jaw, gibbering, divulged
nothing but some new filaments
of blood. For every bloody stroke
with which a frenzied fisherman struck
its head my young son shook his head.
Could I have called out not to look
simply at the one world we shared?
Dead, and examined in detail,
a tarpon's bulk grows beautiful.

Bronze, with a brass-green mould, the scales
age like a corselet of coins,
a net of tarnished silver joins
the back's deep-sea blue to the tail's
wedged, tapering Y.
Set in a stone, triangular skull,
ringing with gold, the open eye
is simply, tiringly there.
A shape so simple, like a cross,
a child could draw it in the air.
A tarpon's scale, its skin's flake
washed at the sea's edge and held
against the light looks just like what
the grinning fisherman said it would:
dense as frost glass but delicate,

etched by a diamond, it showed
a child's drawing of a ship,
the sails' twin triangles, a mast.

Can such complexity of shape,
such bulk, terror and fury fit
in a design so innocent,
that through opaque, phantasmal mist,
moving, but motionlessly, it
sails where imagination sent?

Missing The Sea

Something removed roars in the ears of this house,
Hangs its drapes windless, stuns mirrors
Till reflections lack substance.

Some sound like the gnashing of windmills ground
To a dead halt;
A deafening absence, a blow.

It hoops this valley, weighs this mountain,
Estranges gesture, pushes this pencil
Through a thick nothing now,

Freights cupboards with silence, folds sour laundry
Like the clothes of the dead left exactly
As the dead behaved by the beloved,

Incredulous, expecting occupancy.

The Glory Trumpeter

Old Eddie's face, wrinkled with river lights,
Looked like a Mississippi man's. The eyes,
Derisive and avuncular at once,
Swivelling, fixed me. They'd seen
Too many wakes, too many cat-house nights.
The bony, idle fingers on the valves
Of his knee-cradled horn could tear
Through 'Georgia On My Mind' or 'Jesus Saves'
With the same fury of indifference
If what propelled such frenzy was despair.

Now, as the eyes sealed in the ashen flesh,
And Eddie, like a deacon at his prayer,
Rose, tilting the bright horn, I saw a flash
Of gulls and pigeons from the dunes of coal
Near my grandmother's barracks on the wharves,
I saw the sallow faces of those men
Who sighed as if they spoke into their graves
About the negro in America. That was when
The Sunday comics, sprawled out on her floor,
Sent from the States, had a particular odour;
Dry smell of money mingled with man's sweat.

And yet, if Eddie's features held our fate,
Secure in childhood I did not know then
A jesus-ragtime or gut-bucket blues
To the bowed heads of lean, compliant men
Back from the States in their funereal serge

Black, rusty Homburgs and limp waiters' ties,
Slow, honey accents and lard-coloured eyes
Was Joshua's ram's horn wailing for the Jews
Of patient bitterness or bitter seige.

Now it was that, as Eddie turned his back
On our young crowd out fêteing, swilling liquor,
And blew, eyes closed, one foot up, out to sea,
His horn aimed at those cities of the Gulf,
Mobile and Galveston, and sweetly meted
Their horn of plenty through his bitter cup,
In lonely exaltation blaming me
For all whom race and exile have defeated,
For my own uncle in America,
That living there I never could look up.

Goats and Monkeys

*... even now, an old black ram
is tupping your white ewe.*
Othello

The owl's torches gutter. Chaos clouds the globe.
Shriek, augury! His earthen bulk
buries her bosom in its slow eclipse.
His smoky hand has charred
that marble throat. Bent to her lips,
he is Africa, a vast, sidling shadow
that halves your world with doubt.
'Put out the light', and God's light is put out.

That flame extinct, she contemplates her dream
of him as huge as night, as bodiless,
as starred with medals, like the moon
a fable of blind stone.
Dazzled by that bull's bulk against the sun
of Cyprus, couldn't she have known
like Pasiphaë, poor girl, she'd breed horned monsters?
That like Euyridice, her flesh a flare
travelling the hellish labyrinth of his mind
his soul would swallow hers?

Her white flesh rhymes with night. She climbs, secure.

Virgin and ape, maid and malevolent Moor,
their immoral coupling still halves our world.
He is your sacrificial beast, bellowing, goaded,
a black bull snarled in ribbons of its blood.
And yet, whatever fury girded
on that saffron-sunset turban, moon-shaped sword

was not his racial, panther-black revenge
pulsing her chamber with raw musk, its sweat,
but horror of the moon's change,
of the corruption of an absolute,
like a white fruit
pulped ripe by fondling but doubly sweet.

And so he barbarously arraigns the moon
for all she has beheld since time began
for his own night-long lechery, ambition,
while barren innocence whimpers for pardon.

And it is still the moon, she silvers love,
limns lechery and stares at our disgrace.
Only annihilation can resolve
the pure corruption in her dreaming face.

A bestial, comic agony. We harden
with mockery at this blackamoor
who turns his back on her, who kills
what, like the clear moon, cannot abhor
her element, night; his grief
farcically knotted in a handkerchief
a sibyl's
prophetically stitched remembrancer
webbed and embroidered with the zodiac,
this mythical, horned beast who's no more
monstrous for being black.

The Prince

Genderers of furies, crouching, slavering beasts
those paps that gave me suck! His dragonish scales
are velvet-sheathed, even at those feasts
of coiling tongues. Lust has not soured
that milky stomach. Something more than love
my father lacked which God will not approve:

a savage, sundering sword, vile to the touch
breeding fidelity by its debauch.
Calm, she reclines on her maternal couch,
knitting revenge and lechery in my head.
I ease the sword, and, like her victim, quaking,
I, in my father, stalk my father's dread.

The Wedding of an Actress

Entering from the glare
Of the mid-morning traffic, we assume
Our lily-bordered pew; our eyes
Gradually grow familiar with the gloom.
I recognize that dais
Branching with candles as the stage, the smiles
Exchanged between the carved and living face,
That altar tapestry's archaic zeal
Of harvest, and at the crowd's
Slow scything at the knee, I kneel.

Knowing I am a guest in the Lord's house,
I seal my sense in darkness to admit
That moment where irreconcilables knit
'in a white rose, shaped from the soldiery
which, with His own blood, Christ hath made His spouse.
I press my forehead hard on the scarred pews,
Wrestle with prayer and fail.
It is no use.
In any church my brain is a charred vault
Where demons roost,
A blackened, shifting dust.

A kyrie shrills, hysterical as the ghost
Of a dead marriage in the ear. Nothing is real,
Through my own fault, through my most grievous fault.

And nothing swarms the sight
Until the choir, altering its mood,
Proclaims the bride. The bride. To its diapason,
Between banked lilies and the hallowed stone,
A crystal of calm blood,
Sails her veiled body evenly as the swan,
White as Ophelia on the black flood.

II
We too are actors, who behold
This ceremony; we hold
Our breath, defying dissolution,
Faith, we were told, like art,
Feeds on illusion.

III
Through the illusion of another life,
I can observe this custom like a ghost,
Watching the incense snaking overhead
Dissolving like the wafer laid
In wine along the tongue,
Hearing their promise buried in this vault,
Their lines drowned in the surges of a song.
Yet whether faith or custom matters most,
In each the private tragedy is lost.
Faith is as virginal as every bride,
Custom the church from which I am divorced
Because of pride, because of grievous pride.

Laventville

(for V. S. Naipaul)

To find the Western Path
Through the Gates of Wrath
Blake

It huddled there
steel tinkling its blue painted metal air,
tempered in violence, like Rio's favelas,

with snaking, perilous streets whose edges fell as
its episcopal turkey-buzzards fall
from its miraculous hilltop

shrine,
down the impossible drop
to Belmont, Woodbrook, Maraval, St Clair

that shine
like peddlers' tin trinkets in the sun.
From a harsh

shower, its gutters growled and gargled wash
past the Youth Centre, past the water catchment,
a rigid children's carousel of cement;

we climbed where lank electric
lines and tension cables linked its raw brick
hovels like a complex feud,

where the inheritors of the middle passage stewed
five to a room, still clamped below their hatch,
breeding like felonies,

whose lives revolve round prison, graveyard, church.
Below bent breadfruit trees
in the flat, coloured city, class

lay escalated into structures still,
merchant, middleman, magistrate, knight. To go downhill
from here was to ascend.

The middle passage never guessed its end.
This is the height of poverty
for the desperate and black;

climbing, we could look back
with widening memory
on the hot, corrugated iron sea
whose horrors we all

shared. The salt blood knew it well,
you, me, Samuel's daughter, Samuel,
and those ancestors clamped below its grate.

And climbing steeply past the wild
gutters, it shrilled
in the blood, for those who suffered, who were killed,

and who survive.
What other gift was there to give
as the godparents of his unnamed child?

Yet outside the brown annexe of the church, the
stifling odour of bay rum and talc, the particular,
neat sweetness of the crowd distressed

that sense. The black, fawning verger
his bow tie akimbo, grinning, the clown-gloved
fashionable wear of those I deeply loved

once, made me look on with hopelessness and rage
at their new, apish habits, their excess
and fear, the possessed, the self-possessed;

their perfume shrivelled to a childhood fear
of Sabbath graveyards, christenings, marriages,
that muggy, steaming, self-assuring air

of tropical Sabbath afternoons. And in
the church, eyes prickling with rage,
the children rescued from original sin

by their God-father since the middle passage,
the supercilious brown curate, who intones,

healing the guilt in these rachitic bones,
twisting my love within me like a knife,
'across the troubled waters of this life ... '

Which of us cares to walk
even if God wished
those retching waters where our souls were fished

for this new world? Afterwards, we talk
in whispers, close to death
among these stones planted on alien earth.

Afterwards,
the ceremony, the careful photograph
moved out of range before the patient tombs,

we dare a laugh,
ritual, desperate words,
born like these children from habitual wombs,

from lives fixed in the unalterable groove
of grinding poverty. I stand out on a balcony
and watch the sun pave its flat, golden path

across the roofs, the aerials, cranes, the tops
of fruit trees crawling downward to the city.
Something inside is laid wide like a wound,

some open passage that has cleft the brain,
some deep, amnesiac blow. We left
somewhere a life we never found,

customs and gods that are not born again,
some crib, some grill of light
clanged shut on us in bondage, and withheld

us from that world below us and beyond,
and in its swaddling cerements we're still bound.

The Almond Trees

There's nothing here
this early;
cold sand
cold churning ocean, the Atlantic,
no visible history,

except this stand
of twisted, coppery, sea-almond trees
their shining postures surely
bent as metal, and one

foam-haired, salt-grizzled fisherman,
his mongrel growling, whirling on the stick
he pitches him; its spinning rays
'no visible history'
until their lengthened shapes amaze the sun.

By noon,
this further shore of Africa is strewn
with the forked limbs of girls toasting their flesh
in scarves, sunglasses, Pompeian bikinis,

brown daphnes, laurels, they'll all have
like their originals, their sacred grove,
this frieze
of twisted, coppery, sea-almond trees.

The fierce acetylene air
has singed
their writhing trunks with rust, the same
hues as a foundered, peeling barge.
It'll sear a pale skin copper with its flame.

The sand's white-hot ash underheel,
but their aged limbs have got their brazen sheen
from fire. Their bodies fiercely shine!
They're cured,
they endured their furnace.

Aged trees and oiled limbs share a common colour!

Welded in one flame,
huddling naked, stripped of their name,
for Greek or Roman tags, they were lashed
raw by wind, washed
out with salt and fire-dried,
bitterly nourished where their branches died,

their leaves' broad dialect a coarse,
enduring sound
they shared together.

Not as some running hamadryad's cries
rooted, broke slowly into leaf
her nipples peaking to smooth, wooden boles

Their grief
howls seaward through charred, ravaged holes.

One sunburnt body now acknowledges
that past and its own metamorphosis
as, moving from the sun, she kneels to spread
her wrap within the bent arms of this grove
that grieves in silence, like parental love.

Veranda

(for Ronald Bryden)

Grey apparitions at veranda ends
like smoke, divisible, but one
your age is ashes, its coherence gone,

Planters whose tears were marketable gum, whose voices
scratch the twilight like dried fronds
edged with reflection,

Colonels, hard as the commonwealth's greenheart,
middlemen, usurers whose art
kept an empire in the red,

Upholders of Victoria's china seas
lapping embossed around a drinking mug,
bully-boy roarers of the Empire club,

To the tarantara of the bugler, the sunset furled
round the last post,
the 'flamingo colours' of a fading world,

A ghost steps from you, my grandfather's ghost!
Uprooted from some rainy English shire,
you sought your Roman

End in suicide by fire.
Your mixed son gathered your charred, blackened bones,
in a child's coffin.

And buried them himself on a strange coast.
Sire,
why do I raise you up? Because

Your house has voices, your burnt house,
shrills with unguessed, lovely inheritors,
your genealogical roof tree, fallen, survives,
like seasoned timber through green, little lives.

I ripen towards your twilight, sir, that dream
where I am singed in that sea-crossing, steam
towards that vaporous world, whose souls,

like pressured trees brought diamonds out of coals.
The sparks pitched from your burning house are stars.
I am the man my father loved and was.

Whatever love you suffered makes amends
within them, father.
I climb the stair

And stretch a darkening hand to greet those friends
who share with you the last inheritance
of earth, our shrine and pardoner,

grey, ghostly loungers at veranda ends.

Statues

Stone will not bleed;
Nor shall this vizor'd prince, apotheosized
On his stone steed,
A barrel-bellied charger treading air,
Its tightening haunches set
To hurdle with its warrior the chasm
Between our age and theirs.
Its eyes erupt, bulge in a spasm
Of marble. We stare
At their slow power to corrupt;

Then turn to read
Around another statue, civic-sized,
Bare, balding head,
Of some archaic, muscular aphorist
Laurelled, toga unkempt,
His forked hand raised like a diviner's rod,
His face creased with the wise
Exhaustion of a god.
Their eyes
Withhold amusement, mine, contempt.

Boys will be boys.
Who can instruct them where true honour lies?
Instinct or choice,
Proclaims it lies within
War's furious, dandiacal discipline.
We, who have known

Its victims huddled in a reeking ditch,
Of the shaft's iron light hurtling Saul
Into pedestrian sainthood at his fall,
Still praise that murderous energy of stone.

On them, your fatherly, exhausted air
Is lost,
As sightless as the god's prophetic stare.

Across that gulf each greets the other's ghost.

A Map of Europe

Like Leonardo's idea
Where landscapes open on a waterdrop
Or dragons crouch in stains,
My flaking wall, in the bright air,
Maps Europe with its veins.

On its limned window ledge
A beer can's gilded rim gleams like
Evening along a Canaletto lake,
Or like that rocky hermitage
Where, in his cell of light, haggard Jerome
Prays that His kingdom come
To the far city.

The light creates its stillness. In its ring
Everything IS. A cracked coffee cup,
A broken loaf, a dented urn become
Themselves, as in Chardin,
Or in beer-bright Vermeer,
Not objects of our pity.

In it is no lacrimae rerum,
No art. Only the gift
To see things as they are, halved by a darkness
From which they cannot shift.

Nights in the Gardens of Port of Spain

Night, our black summer, simplifies her smells
into a village; she assumes the impenetrable

musk of the Negro, grows secret as sweat,
her alleys odorous with shucked oyster shells,

coals of gold oranges, braziers of melon.
Commerce and tambourines increase her heat.

Hellfire or the whorehouse: crossing Park Street,
a surf of sailors' faces crests, is gone

with the sea's phosphorescence; the boîtes de nuit
twinkle like fireflies in her thick hair.

Blinded by headlamps, deaf to taxi klaxons,
she lifts her face from the cheap, pitch-oil flare

towards white stars, like cities, flashing neon,
burning to be the bitch she will become.

As daylight breaks the Indian turns his tumbril
of hacked, beheaded coconuts towards home.

God Rest Ye Merry Gentlemen

Splitting from Jack Delaney's, Sheridan Square,
that winter night, stewed, seasoned in bourbon,
my body kindled by the whistling air
snowing the Village that Christ was reborn,
I lurched like any lush by his own glow
across towards Sixth, and froze before the tracks
of footprints bleeding on the virgin snow.
I tracked them where they led across the street
to the bright side, entering the wax-
sealed smell of neon, human heat,
some all-night diner with its wise-guy cook
his stub thumb in my bowl of stew and one
man's pulped and beaten face, its look
acknowledging all that, white-dark outside,
was possible: some beast prowling the block,
something fur-clotted, running wild
beyond the boundary of will. Outside,
more snow had fallen. My heart charred.
I longed for darkness, evil that was warm.
Walking, I'd stop and turn. What had I heard,
wheezing behind my heel with whitening breath?
Nothing. Sixth Avenue yawned wet and wide.
The night was white. There was nowhere to hide.

November Sun

In our treacherous
seasonless climate's
dry heat or muggy heat or rain
I'm measuring winter by this November sun's
diagonals shafting the window pane,
by my crouched shadow's
embryo on the morning study-floor. Once

I wallowed in ignorance
of change, of windfall, snowfall,
skull-cracking heat, sea-threshing hurricane.
Now I'd prefer to know.
We age desiring
these icy intuitions
that seasons bring.

Look, they'll be pierced with knowledge
as with light! One boy, nine years in age
who vaults and tumbles, squirrelling
in his perpetual spring,
that ten-month, cautious totterer
my daughter.
I rarely let them in.

This is a sort of
death cell
where knowledge of our fatality is hidden.
I trace here, like a bent astronomer

the circle of the year,
nurturing its inner seasons'
mulch, drench, fire, ash.
In my son's
restless gaze
I am time-ridden,
the sedentary dial of his days.
Our shadows point one way,
even their brief shadows on the cropped morning grass.

I am pierced with this. I cannot look away.
Ah Christ, how cruelly the needles race!

'O Trees of Life, What are Your Signs of Winter?'

(for E.S.)

Her passion was for objects, the sane life
Displayed like crystal on blond oak,
Bowls, spatulas, snowy linen.
So, suddenly, when he died,
She wanted this blue vase
They'd seen in a show-window.
When I brought it, she said,
Her vision glazed with shock:
'Place this on a ledge
in winter, it irradiates Stockholm.'
Distracted? Our knowledge
Revolves in a blue sphere.
Passionate of breath
We cloud a little dome.

So I imagine her
This winter at a window,
Shawled, in an empty room
With two forgetting children,
In the blue globe I brought
Her when he died, her thought
Whirled rootlessly like snow.

Lines in New England

'The cruel lie of caste refute,
Old forms remould, and substitute
For Slavery's lash the freeman's will,
For blind routine, wise-handed skill;
A school-house plant on every hill,
Stretching in radiate nerve-lines thence
The quick wires of intelligence;
Till North and South together brought
Shall own the same electric thought,
In peace a common flag salute,
And, side by side in labour's free
And unresentful rivalry,
Harvest the fields wherein they fought!'–Whither: Snowbound

Geese creaking south, a raucous
chain unlocking winter's cavernous
barn, cross me
going the other way.
Why am I so far north,
who dread these stripped trees' polar
iron, and fear fall,
cinders and brimstone of
the pilgrim's prophecy? I look
from arrowing train lines at the track
this crabbed hand makes, at every trick
of its shot trade. It runs, cramped
from itself with loathing: the pumped
detonation under sulphurous

sheets, the white, treacherous
hands it has been gripped by;
a crab wallowing in the water of
a salt, warm, drifting eye;
the breasts it's held in love,
in hollow love. The ruled lie
it follows. Yet not once has this hand
sought to strike home. Outside,
an Indian summer whose trees radiate
like veins, a salt-blue pond,
where I imagine a crazed, single, deer-
skinned quarry drinking, the last
Mohican. Redcoat, redman, their thirst-
ing, autumn battle-ground,
its savage lacerations healed
by salt white spire and green field.
I watch from my side of the glass
the lantern slides clicking across
the window glazed by ocean air.
Mine, or another history there?
A civilization with its dreams
of guilt; the trails drive grittily,
their power clamps the jaw
tight with abhorrence and with love
these parallels, that seem to move
to blue infinity, laid down the law
of separate but equal love.

The Voyage Up River

(for Wilson Harris)

They roll as deaf as logs through foliage swollen
With elephantiasis to the green screech of macaws;

This is their second death, and they have fallen
All over, overboard, swirling like oars.

Does the piranha shred their bones of flesh
Again, boiled in the tide-race,

And the scaled cayman heave its hulk and flash
To halve their limbs in the original place?

On that vague expedition did their souls
Spawn, vaporous as butterflies, in resurrection,

Or the small terrors multiply like tadpoles
Below a mangrove root or a headstone?

Stillborn in death, their memory is not ours,
In whom the spasm of birth

Gendered oblivion. To chart empty savannahs,
Rivers, even with a guide, conceives an earth

Without us, without gods: Guiana or Guinea,
An aboriginal fear, lie Orinoco

Disgorging from a mouth brown with tobacco
Deaths that cannot discolour the great sea.

Crusoe's Journal

I looked now upon the world as a thing remote, which I had nothing
to do with, no expectation from, and, indeed no desires about. In a
word, I had nothing indeed to do with it, nor was ever like to have;
so I thought it looked as we may perhaps look upon it hereafter, viz.,
as a place I had lived in but was come out of it; and well might I say,
as Father Abraham to Dives, 'Between me and thee is a great gulf fixed.'

Robinson Crusoe

Once we have driven past Mundo Nuevo trace
      safely to this beach house
perched between ocean and green, churning forest
      the intellect appraises
objects surely, even the bare necessities
      of style are turned to use,
like those plain iron tools he salvages
      from shipwreck, hewing a prose
as odorous as raw wood to the adze,
      out of such timbers
came our first book, our profane Genesis
      whose Adam speaks that prose
which, blessing some sea-rock, startles itself
      with poetry's surprise,
in a green world, one without metaphors;
      like Christofer he bears
in speech mnemonic as a missionary's
      the Word to savages,
its shape an earthen, water-bearing vessel's
      whose sprinkling alters us
into good Fridays who recite His praise,
      parroting our master's
style and voice, we make his language ours,
      converted cannibals
we learn with him to eat the flesh of Christ.

All shapes, all objects multiplied from his,
      our ocean's Proteus;

in childhood, his derelict's old age
        was like a god's. (Now pass
in memory, in serene parenthesis,
        the cliff-deep leeward coast
of my own island filing past the noise
        of stuttering canvas,
some noon-struck village, Choiseul, Canaries,
        with crocodile canoes,
a savage settlement from Henty's novels,
        Marryat or R.L.S.,
with one boy signalling at the sea's edge,
        though what he cried is lost;)
So time that makes us objects, multiplies
        our natural loneliness.

For the hermetic skill, that from earth's clays
        shapes something without use,
and separate from itself, lives somewhere else,
        sharing with every beach
a longing for those gulls that cloud the cays
        with raw, mimetic cries,
never surrenders wholly for it knows
        it needs another's praise
like hoar, half-cracked Ben Gunn, until it cries
        at last, 'O happy desert!'
and learns again the self-creating peace
        of islands. So from this house
that faces nothing but the sea, his journals
        assume a household use,
We learn to shape from them, where nothing was
        the language of a race,
and since the intellect demands its mask
        that sun-cracked, bearded face
provides us with the wish to dramatize
        ourselves at nature's cost,
to attempt a beard, to squint through the sea-haze,
        posing as naturalists,

drunks, castaways, beachcombers, all of us
           yearn for those fantasies
of innocence, for our faith's arrested phase
           when the clear voice
startled itself saying 'water, heaven, Christ,'
           hoarding such heresies as
God's loneliness moves in His smallest creatures.

Crusoe's Island

I

The chapel's cowbell
Like God's anvil
Hammers ocean to a blinding shield;
Fired, the sea-grapes slowly yield
Bronze plates to the metallic heat.

Red, corrugated iron
Roofs roar in the sun.
The wiry, ribbed air
Above earth's open kiln
Writhes like a child's vision
Of hell, but nearer, nearer.

Below, the picnic plaid
Of Scarborough is spread
To a blue, perfect sky,
Dome of our hedonist philosophy.
Bethel and Canaan's heart
Lie open like a psalm.
I labour at my art.
My father, God, is dead.

Past thirty now I know
To love the self is dread
Of being swallowed by the blue
Of heaven overhead
Or rougher blue below.
Some lesion of the brain

From art or alcohol
Flashes this fear by day:
As startling as his shadow
Grows to the castaway.

Upon this rock the bearded hermit built
His Eden:
Goats, corn-crop, fort, parasol, garden,
Bible for sabbath, all the joys
But one
Which sent him howling for a human voice.
Exiled by a flaming sun
The rotting nut, bowled in the surf
Became his own brain rotting from the guilt
Of heaven without his kind,
Crazed by such paradisal calm
The spinal shadow of a palm
Built keel and gunwale in his mind.

The second Adam since the fall
His germinal
Corruption held the seed
Of that congenital heresy that men fail
According to their creed.
Craftsman and castaway
All heaven in his head,
He watched his shadow pray
Not for God's love but human love instead.

II

We came here for the cure
Of quiet in the whelk's centre,
From the fierce, sudden quarrel,
From kitchens where the mind
Like bread, disintegrates in water,
To let a salt sun scour
The brain as harsh as coral
To bathe like stones in wind,
To be, like beast or natural object, pure.

That fabled, occupational
Compassion, supposedly inherited with the gift
Of poetry had fed
With a rat's thrift on faith, shifted
Its trust to corners, hoarded
Its mania like bread,
Its brain a white, nocturnal bloom
That in a drunken, moonlit room
Saw my son's head
Swaddled in sheets
Like a lopped nut, lolling in foam.

O love, we die alone!
I am borne by the bell
Backward to boyhood
To the grey wood
Spire, harvest and marigold,
To those whom a cruel
Just God could gather
To His blue breast, His beard
A folding cloud,
As He gathered my father.
Irresolute and proud,
I can never go back.

I have lost sight of hell,
Of heaven, of human will,
My skill
Is not enough,
I am struck by this bell
To the root.
Crazed by a racking sun,
I stand at my life's noon,
On parched, delirious sand
My shadow lengthens.

III

Art is profane and pagan,

The most it has revealed
Is what a crippled Vulcan
Beat on Achilles' shield.
By these blue, changing graves
Fanned by the furnace blast
Of heaven, may the mind
Catch fire till it cleaves
Its mould of clay at last.

Now Friday's progeny,
The brood of Crusoe's slave,
Black little girls in pink
Organdy, crinolines,
Walk in their air of glory
Beside a breaking wave;
Below their feet the surf
Hisses like tambourines.

At dusk when they return
For vespers, every dress
Touched by the sun will burn
A seraph's, an angel's,
And nothing I can learn
From art or loneliness
Can bless them as the bell's
Transfiguring tongue can bless.

Lampfall

Closest at lampfall
Like children, like the moth-flame metaphor,
The Coleman's humming jet at the sea's edge
A tuning fork for our still family choir
Like Joseph Wright of Derby's astrological lecture
Casts rings of benediction round the aged.
I never tire of ocean's quarrelling,
Its silence, its raw voice,
Nor of these half-lit, windy leaves, gesticulating higher
'Rejoice, rejoice ...'

But there's an old fish, a monster
Of primal fiction that drives barrelling
Undersea, too old to make a splash,
To which I'm hooked!
Through daydream, through nightmare trolling
Me so deep that no lights flash
There but the plankton's drifting, phosphorescent stars.

I see with its aged eyes,
Its dead green, glaucous gaze,
And I'm elsewhere, far as
I shall ever be from you whom I behold now
Dear family, dear friends, by this still glow,
The lantern's ring that the sea's
Never extinguished.
Your voices curl in the shell of my ear.

All day you've watched
The sea-rock like a loom
Shuttling its white wool, sheer Penelope!
The coals lit, the sky glows, an oven.
Heart into heart carefully laid
Like bread.
This is the fire that draws us by our dread
Of loss, the furnace door of heaven.

At night we have heard
The forest, an ocean of leaves, drowning her children,
Still, we belong here. There's Venus. We are not yet lost.

Like you, I preferred
The firefly's starlike little
Lamp, mining, a question,
To the highway's brightly multiplying beetles.

Coral

This coral's shape echoes the hand
It hollowed. Its

Immediate absence is heavy. As pumice,
As your breast in my cupped palm.

Sea-cold, its nipple rasps like sand,
Its pores, like yours, shone with salt sweat.

Bodies in absence displace their weight,
And your smooth body, like none other

Creates an exact absence like this stone
Set on a table with a whitening wrack

Of souvenirs. It dares my hand
To claim what lovers' hands have never known:

The nature of the body of another.

Codicil

Schizophrenic, wrenched by two styles,
one a hack's hired prose, I earn
my exile. I trudge this sickle, moonlit beach for miles,

tan, burn
to slough off
this love of ocean that's self-love.

To change your language you must change your life.

I cannot right old wrongs.
Waves tire of horizon and return.
Gulls screech with rusty tongues

Above the beached, rotting pirogues,
they were a venomous beaked cloud at Charlotteville.

Once I thought love of country was enough,
now, even I chose, there's no room at the trough.

I watch the best minds root like dogs
for scraps of favour.
I am nearing middle-

age, burnt skin
peels from my hand like paper, onion-thin,
like Peer Gynt's riddle.

At heart there's nothing, not the dread
of death. I know too many dead.
They're all familiar, all in character,

even how they died. On fire,
the flesh no longer fears that furnace mouth
of earth,

that kiln or ashpit of the sun,
nor this clouding, unclouding sickle moon
whitening this beach again like a blank page.

All its indifference is a different rage.